MY LEFT NUT

The true story of a Belfast boy growing up
with no father to guide him through, and a
giant ball to weigh him down

by Michael Patrick and Oisín Kearney

samuelfrench.co.uk

FOR AMATEUR PRODUCTION ENQUIRIES

UNITED KINGDOM AND WORLD
EXCLUDING NORTH AMERICA
plays@samuelfrench.co.uk
020 7255 4302/01

Each title is subject to availability from Samuel French,
depending upon country of performance.

THINKING ABOUT PERFORMING A SHOW?

There are thousands of plays and musicals available to perform from Samuel French right now, and applying for a licence is easier and more affordable than you might think

From classic plays to brand new musicals, from monologues to epic dramas, there are shows for everyone.

Plays and musicals are protected by copyright law, so if you want to perform them, the first thing you'll need is a licence. This simple process helps support the playwright by ensuring they get paid for their work and means that you'll have the documents you need to stage the show in public.

Not all our shows are available to perform all the time, so it's important to check and apply for a licence before you start rehearsals or commit to doing the show.

LEARN MORE & FIND THOUSANDS OF SHOWS

Browse our full range of plays and musicals, and find out more about how to license a show
www.samuelfrench.co.uk/perform

Talk to the friendly experts in our Licensing team for advice on choosing a show and help with licensing
plays@samuelfrench.co.uk   020 7387 9373

Acting Editions

BORN TO PERFORM

Playscripts designed from the ground up to work the way you do in rehearsal, performance and study

---

Larger, clearer text for easier reading

Wider margins for notes

Performance features such as character and props lists, sound and lighting cues, and more

---

+ CHOOSE A SIZE AND STYLE TO SUIT YOU

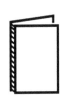

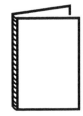

STANDARD EDITION	**SPIRAL-BOUND EDITION**	**LARGE EDITION**
Our regular paperback book at our regular size	The same size as the Standard Edition, but with a sturdy, easy-to-fold, easy-to-hold spiral-bound spine	A4 size and spiral bound, with larger text and a blank page for notes opposite every page of text – perfect for technical and directing use

LEARN MORE | samuelfrench.co.uk/actingeditions

MUSIC USE NOTE

Licensees are solely responsible for obtaining formal written permission from copyright owners to use copyrighted music in the performance of this play and are strongly cautioned to do so. If no such permission is obtained by the licensee, then the licensee must use only original music that the licensee owns and controls. Licensees are solely responsible and liable for all music clearances and shall indemnify the copyright owners of the play(s) and their licensing agent, Samuel French, against any costs, expenses, losses and liabilities arising from the use of music by licensees. Please contact the appropriate music licensing authority in your territory for the rights to any incidental music.

USE OF COPYRIGHT MUSIC

A licence issued by Samuel French Ltd to perform this play does not include permission to use the incidental music specified in this copy.

Where the place of performance is already licensed by the PERFORMING RIGHT SOCIETY (PRS) a return of the music used must be made to them. If the place of performance is not so licensed then application should be made to the PRS, 2 Pancras Square, London, N1C 4AG.

A separate and additional licence from
PHONOGRAPHIC PERFORMANCE LTD,
1 Upper James Street, London W1F 9DE (www.ppluk.com) is needed whenever commercial recordings are used.

IMPORTANT BILLING AND CREDIT REQUIREMENTS

If you have obtained performance rights to this title, please refer to your licensing agreement for important billing and credit requirements.

ABOUT THE AUTHORS

MICHAEL PATRICK

Michael was born and raised in Belfast, where he still lives today. In primary 6, he wrote a story of the nativity from the donkey's perspective and his teacher told his mother that he was going to be a writer. He then went off to study Physics at the University of Cambridge and this is the first thing he has written since then.

Michael usually works as an actor across the UK and Ireland. *My Left Nut* is the (mostly) true story of a period in his teenage years. Some names have been changed to protect the identities of his friends, but most of the genuinely ridiculous events are factual.

As an actor he has worked with the Lyric Theatre Belfast, the Abbey Theatre Dublin, Northern Ireland Opera, the Royal Shakespeare Company and has appeared on *Game of Thrones*, *Krypton*, *Death and Nightingales* and *Soft Border Patrol*.

OISÍN KEARNEY

Oisín is from Warrenpoint, Co. Down. He studied Politics at the University of Cambridge. He now lives in Belfast, where he works as a writer and director for stage and screen.

Oisín localised Willy Russell's script of *Educating Rita* to 1980s Belfast for the Lyric Theatre, and was Assistant Director on the project. He was also Assistant Director on The Lyric's production of *Good Vibrations*, and worked closely with Colin Carberry and Glen Patterson on their translation of the story from screen to stage.

He has directed several documentaries, including *All for Show* (BBC NI True North), *BBeyond* (BBC Arts Show), *Borderlands and Unfinished Revolution* (De Correspondent, NPO2) and *BOJAYÁ: Caught in the Crossfire* (Hot Docs Film Festival 2019).

TOGETHER

Michael and Oisín met at Churchill College, Cambridge, where together they ran the University's Ireland Society and created theatre. For the past number of years they've made theatre in Belfast with their company Pan Narrans Theatre; Michael acting and Oisín directing.

My Left Nut was the first play they wrote together. Their second play, *The Alternative*, was the winner of Fishamble's "A Play for Ireland" initiative, and will premier at the Dublin Theatre Festival in 2019.

AUTHORS' NOTES

If you had told me ten years ago that I would eventually write a play about my swollen testicle and perform it to hundreds of people, there is no way I would have believed you... Back then I hadn't even told my mum.

The whole process has been an absolute privilege. Not only do I get to tell everyone about how great my mum is, and how amazing my dad was. I get to share stories about my brilliant school friends, how stupid and hilarious they all are, and what it was like growing up in Belfast in the early '00s. At the time of writing I've performed the show nearly a hundred times and I'm still excited to perform it every time.

One of the most touching things to have come out of this play is the number of men who have shared similar personal stories with Oisín and myself. Men find it very hard to open up about personal issues, especially testicular ones. It took me three years to pluck up the courage to tell someone about the lump on my testicle. Three years of worry and panic. Thankfully I pulled through, but other people might not be so lucky. So – check your balls, and talk to people.

I'd love to thank everyone who helped us get to this point, but particularly Oisín. I wouldn't have trusted anyone else to help write my story. I think we are very lucky that we work so well together, and I'm very proud of what we have created. Even if it does mean the chancer is profiting from my childhood trauma.

Michael Patrick, Co-author and original performer

AUTHORS' NOTES

It was a daunting prospect to co-write and direct a play about Michael's testicular problem and the loss of his father, but we trusted each other and shared a common vision of creating a comedy out of the most secret of issues. Realising Michael's ability to conjure up the audience's imagination through high-energy physical comedy, we stripped away all props except for a single chair.

It has been a challenge to direct a friend in a one-man show based on his own experience, but to facilitate the telling of a heart-warming and hilarious story in a compelling way is, for me, what this theatre craic is all about. Even if it does mean putting up with Mick's fragile ego and incredibly annoying face.

Oisín Kearney, Co-author and original director

My Left Nut was developed as part of *Show in a Bag*, an artist development initiative of Dublin Fringe, Fishamble: The New Play Company and Irish Theatre Institute to resource theatre makers and actors. Additional support was provided through Prime Cut Productions' *Reveal* programme.

First performed at Bewley's Café Theatre at the Dublin Fringe Festival, September 2017:

Performer	Michael Patrick
Director	Oisín Kearney
Mentor	Emma Jordan
Stage Manager	Colm Maher
Script Development	Gavin Kostick
Movement	Jude Quinn

Followed by an Irish tour and Edinburgh Festival Fringe run in 2018, co-produced by Pan Narrans Theatre and Prime Cut Productions, supported by Culture Ireland:

Performer	Michael Patrick
Director	Oisín Kearney
Stage Managers	Ashley Smyth
	Gina Donnelly
	Ross McDade
Producers	Stephen Coulter
	Una NicEoin

ACKNOWLEDGEMENTS

This is the first play we've written and we couldn't have got it this far without the help and support of so many brilliant people.

Gavin Kostick, Jim Culleton, Eva Scanlan, Siobhán Bourke, Jane Daly, Eláine Donnelly, Ruth McGowan, Kris Nelson and everyone else at Fishamble, the Dublin Fringe Festival and the Irish Theatre Institute for accepting us onto *Show in a Bag* and giving us the push to create the play.

Emma Jordan, Una NicEoin, Stephen Coulter, Gina Donnelly, Ross McDade, Ashley Smyth and all at Prime Cut for supporting us through their *Reveal* programme.

Róise Goan, Sam O'Mahony, Fionnuala Kennedy, Sarah Gordon, Caoileann Curry-Thompson, Rhiann Jeffrey, Lisa Dwyer Hogg and all at the Tyrone Guthrie Centre in Annaghmakerrig where we frantically rewrote the play in a long weekend.

Colm Maher, David Horan and Bewley's Café Theatre, Jude Quinn, Simon Magill, Stuart Campbell, The MAC, Accidental Theatre, Tom Forster, Robert McDowell, Summerhall, Ciaran Walsh, Culture Ireland, Cáit Fahey, Peter Murray and all the amazing theatres, festivals and audiences around Ireland who supported the show.

Thanks to all of Michael's family and friends who not only let us tell their story, but provided incredible support and assistance throughout the whole project; specifically Pauline Campbell, Kate Campbell, Maurice Campbell, Hannah Campbell, Naomi Sheehan, and the lads who provided the inspiration for Tommy and Conor.

CHARACTER LIST

All characters to be played by one actor.
No costume or props used to indicate different characters,
just vocal and physical changes.
MICK *and* YOUNG MICK *both talk to the audience and inhabit*
the scenes they are in.
No other characters talk to the audience.

MICK – An awkward teenager.
YOUNG MICK – Mick as an eight-year-old child.
MOTHER – Mick's mother, Pauline Campbell.
UNCLE – Mick's uncle.
MAURICE – Mick's younger brother.
SISTER – Mick's sister.
TOMMY – Mick's friend from school. Loud and boisterous.
CONOR – Mick's friend from school. Slower.
DOCTOR – Consultant in hospital.
NURSE – An overworked nurse.
ULTRASOUND MAN – An ultrasound technician. Brash.
BUS DRIVER – A person who drives the bus.
NIAL THE NUTTER – Teenage party-goer.
SIOBHAN – Teenage party-goer.
MARY – Teenage party-goer.
CAHIL – Eighteen-year-old from the countryside.
TOMMY'S DA – Tommy's father.

Change is used to indicate a change in time/place.
They are often very quick and sharp, but some can be
given time.
They may be accompanied by a lighting or sound cue, but
not always.

Some specific sound cues are written in, and should be
used when indicated. All other cues are left to the director's
discretion.

*Dedicated to Michael Damien Thaddeus Campbell,
who died too young*

*And to Pauline Patricia Campbell, who couldn't bring
him back for us, but who did everything else*

A single chair in the middle of an otherwise empty stage. The chair has a school tie over the back of it, and a pair of old trainers leaning up against it. Over the following VOICEOVER, MICK *walks out and sits in the chair. He is wearing a white shirt, black trousers, and socks.*

A VOICEOVER *from a real-life news report plays.*

VOICE OVER From Castle Buildings at Stormont outside Belfast on the day of a truly momentous agreement, promising a fundamental change between north and south and between Britain and Ireland.

MICK *talks to the audience.*

MICK Belfast. 1998. D'you remember? Talks, talks, talks. A long hard slog towards a fragile peace. But tensions were still high. Paramilitaries still refusing to give up their weapons. A stand-off with 10,000 Orangemen on the Garvaghy Road. 29 people killed in Omagh. D'you remember that? D'you know what I remember? I remember the look on mum's face. When she told me—

Change.

MOTHER Dad's dead.

YOUNG MICK No he's not.

MOTHER I'm sorry Michael.

Change.

The opening music to the Sega Mega Drive/Genesis game Streets of Rage* plays.

---

* A licence to produce MY LEFT NUT does not include a performance licence for "STREETS OF RAGE". For further information, please see Music Use Note on page v.

MICK This city was once a happy peaceful place...until one day, a powerful secret criminal organisation took over. The city has become a centre of violence and crime where no one is safe. Amid this turmoil, a group of determined young police officers have sworn to clean up the city. They are willing to risk anything, even their lives...on the... STREETS OF RAGE! SEGA!

Change.

YOUNG MICK *(to audience)* Streets of rage! Playing as Adam Hunter, twenty-three-year-old black ex-cop with a vicious right hook. Cleaning up the streets in sixteen-bit colour. Ignoring everything around me as I stayed locked into the neon world of the Sega Mega Drive!

Get him, get him, get him!

MOTHER Michael. Turn that off. It's time to go.

Change.

YOUNG MICK *(reads)* Michael Damien Thaddeus Campbell. Died 15th October 1998, aged forty-seven. Do Not Let Your Hearts Be Troubled. *(to audience)* I watch my dad's coffin being lowered into the ground. It's not my dad anyway. It's just a body. Dad's away on.

UNCLE Here's the man of the house now.

Change (now fifteen-year-old MICK*).*

Over the following speech MICK *puts on his old trainers.*

MICK I was eight years old. My elder sister was nine, my younger brother was three, and my baby sister was sixteen months. Mum had to go get a job. She found work as a priest's housekeeper and we all called her Mrs Doyle. We lived in South Belfast. Went for walks on the Lagan Towpath. Went to Donegal every Twelfth of July. And mostly...mostly I just hung out with my mates, talking bollocks.

Change.

TOMMY Here. Do ever stick your finger up your bum?

MICK What?!

MICK *puts on the school tie, which was on the chair.*

(to audience) I'm fifteen. Secondary school. Mates. Hormones going mental. Sense of self bouncing all over the show. Who am I? What's my place in the world? Am I straight? Am I gay? Am I cool?! And my main connection to the world of masculinity and manliness is this group of beautifully cocky terrified boys. I love them.

TOMMY No, seriously. I was up in the *gaeltacht* last summer, right?

MICK *(to audience)* Tommy. He lives in West Belfast and we all think his da's in the IRA. Because one time we found a box full of balaclavas hidden underneath their stairs.

TOMMY And I'm getting with this girl. She's an absolute beauty. Speaks Irish and all. Sure I haven't a clue. And one night, we're sitting in her dad's field, and we must've drank like three full bottles of vodka...each!

CONOR There's no way you can drink three bottles of vodka, Tommy. You'd die.

MICK *(to audience)* Conor. He's our authority on girls because he actually has a girlfriend. She goes to an all-girls' school in Newry. We've never met her.

CONOR You'd literally die, Tommy. Stop spoofing!

TOMMY Yeah yeah. I know...but this is Free State vodka. It's weaker. Like ya know how the Dairy Milk is different down there? It's the same thing. So, there we were, and things start to get a bit hot and heavy, if you know what I mean. And she starts making all of these Irish sex noises!

CONOR What does that even mean?!

TOMMY They're like regular sex noises, Conor, but they're more free. They're less oppressed by the yoke of the British Empire. Now, I don't have a clue what she's saying, but it's guttural or something. Speaks to me on a mythical level. She asks me a question. I just nod my head. I can't even speak, I'm in that much ecstasy. And next thing I know…she shoves her finger right up my hole!

MICK What?! In your bum. That's stinkin.

TOMMY Mick, I'm telling you. It was unbelievable. I'm addicted. So now like once, maybe twice a week, I sit down and really treat myself. I put on some Sinead O'Conor and explore the depths of my rectum.

MICK Oh right.

Change.

(to audience) Now, I know Tommy's just running his mouth. He gets hammered on half a bottle of WKD. He can barely get up the courage to speak to a girl, let alone all that other stuff. But maybe he's onto something. I mean, if Tommy's doing it. Maybe everyone's doing it. And if everyone's doing it, I don't want to be the one weirdo who's not doing it. *(beat)* I'm testing out the back-door system!

Change.

Seated and with his back to the audience, **MICK** *lowers his trousers (but not his boxers) to his ankles and masturbates. He raises one hand with his finger extended, slouches down in his chair and raises both legs. He moves his finger down between his legs. As he brushes past his testicles, he stops in his tracks and slams his feet to the ground and stands up.*

The whole sequence should be over-the-top and done in time to upbeat music (Hot 8 Brass Band, Sexual Healing – or similar).

(to audience) What's that? Is that a lump? It's only on one of them. Was that always there? *(pause)* Ach, I just need to finish.

MICK *goes back to wanking.*

Céad Míle Fáilte... Radió na Gaeltachta... TG Ceathair... SAM MAGUIRE!

MAURICE　Mick! What are you doing? You're shaking the bunk bed.

MICK　Nothing, Maurice! Shut up! Go back to sleep.

(to audience) It's tough sharing a room with your wee brother when you're a teenager. Especially when you find a lump on your ball. It starts small. Just a little bump. I don't know what it is. It must have something to do with... *(makes masturbating motion)* Like, you're not supposed to do that. It's a sin! Well, I don't really believe in all that, but still... I'm not telling Mum. And over the next year, it gets bigger and bigger and bigger. But there is so much else going on! I start getting hair on my upper lip. I need an ACTUAL shave, before it turns into a dirty smick tash. I know how to shave. There's an episode of The Simpsons where Homer teaches Bart how to shave. I watched that like a million times. Until...

Change.

Well, Mother. What's going on?

MOTHER　What's going on? I'm ironing. I swear, the amount of ironing in this house.

MICK　Cool. Nice. You going to the shops today?

MOTHER　Aye. I'll be going to the big Tesco's. Why? Have we run out of KitKats?

MICK　No. I was just wondering if you could get me some... shaving stuff.

Pause.

MOTHER Shaving stuff?

MICK Yeah, you know. Just need to shave...

MOTHER Oh right. Right. Aye. Well. That's not a problem. What sort of shaving stuff do you need?

MICK WHAT'S WITH ALL THE QUESTIONS MUM, I JUST NEED TO SHAVE?!

MOTHER RIGHT OK RIGHT RIGHT! I'll have it for you after school!

Change.

MICK *(to audience)* I meet up with the lads in the usual spot. *(to the lads)* Well, lads. What's the craic?

CONOR Apparently Tommy has discovered the secret to picking up women.

MICK What's that, Tommy? Don't be ugly as sin?

TOMMY Ugly as sin? That's not what your ma said last night. Yeoooo!

CONOR Yeeooooo!

TOMMY No. It's about group dynamics. I've been reading all about it. You need lads who complement each other. Conor, you're the Looks, right. Me, I'm the Charmer. And Mick's the Stallion.

MICK What do you mean I'm the Stallion?

CONOR Stop trying to be modest. We all know you're packin.

TOMMY Come on, Mick. You can see it through your trousers! You've got some equipment there!

MICK Piss off, lads!

TOMMY Woah! It's a good thing. Every group's gotta have one lad with a big dick it in. Gives us prestige. Fair play!

Change.

MICK *(to audience)* So, the lads have noticed the bulge. I've been trying to hide it... Getting changed in PE has become pretty awkward. It actually fell out of my shorts one time in PE, when we were doing sprints. Thankfully the fella behind me was so traumatised by what he saw swinging there in front of his eyes, he didn't tell anyone. I mean, I still haven't told anyone. It'll probably go away on its own... I run home from school, so excited to get my new razor. Nice clean lines. Soap. Lather. Shave. Clean. Sharp. Manly. I burst in the door.

Change.

MOTHER Michael! I got you your razor! It's one of them electric ones!

MICK An electric one? What?

MOTHER You just turn it on and away you go. Don't need to worry about... I mean... I just thought it'd be handy.

MICK Do you not think I can be trusted with a blade?

MOTHER What? No! The man at the shop said they were very popular.

MICK Do you think I'm an idiot? Do you think I'm a fucking child?

MOTHER Michael! Don't disrespect me like that.

MICK Why the fuck should I respect you? I hate you.

Silence.

You don't know what you're doing. DO YOU?

Silence.

(to audience) I storm out. The razor with me. Run into the bathroom and slam the door behind me.

Change.

(to audience) I look into the mirror. My face is flushed red. I've never spoken to Mum like that before.

MICK *turns on electric razor. It buzzes. He turns it off.*

(to audience) It's a big dull beast of a thing! Not slick. Not sharp. Not what a man uses. I don't see a man. I see an angry child. My dad was never angry. I remember he told me: never use the word "hate", unless you're talking about Margaret Thatcher. Otherwise that word was only for people who can't admit they're afraid.

Dad? I am afraid. It's not cancer, is it? Testicular cancer. That's the one you get young.

Change.

(to audience) Something has to change. I'm the man of the house! And a man takes his destiny into his own hands. I try everything. I try draining it. I try squeezing it. I try having cold showers. Hot baths. Moisturiser. Deep heat. Ice packs. Dipping it in the holy water from Lourdes! Nothing worked. It was time to do some research.

Change.

MICK *sits at computer as dial-up internet noise plays.*

(types) Ask Jeeves... What causes swollen testicles? *(reads)* "Swollen testicles can be caused by testicular torsion. This condition causes the testicle to twist inside the scrotum and is considered a medical emergency. Testicular torsion can disrupt the blood supply to the testicle and may even cause tissue death... Shit! Images. Images.

(to audience) I wait in front of the computer, as the image slowly loads. Line...by line...by Line...

MSN notification noise.

The lads are on MSN! *(reads)* Waaaassssssssssup? *(types)* Waaaassssssssssup?

MSN notification noise.

(reads) Tommy: FREE GAFF NEXT WEEK! *(to audience)* Yes! Free gaff, free gaff! *(types)* U gettin drink?

Two MSN notification noises.

(reads) Conor: my culchie cousin's just turned eighteen, he'll sort it. *(reads)* Tommy: We r gunna be swimmin in pussssssssaaaaaaaay!!!! *(types)* Tommy...we don't know any girls.

SISTER It's my turn, Mick, hurry up! You've been on for ages!

MICK *(to audience)* I quickly exit out of MSN to hide my illicit plans from my sister. She stops in her tracks. Her jaw falls to the floor. Her eyes widen in shock. I look at the screen. And there it is...fully loaded!

SISTER MUM! MICHAEL'S LOOKING AT PICTURES OF PRIVATE PARTS!

Change.

MICK Wank. Cry. Sleep.

Change.

Mum.

MOTHER What's wrong. What do you want?

MICK I have...doesn't matter.

MOTHER Ach no. Something's up with you. What is it?

MICK How did Dad first know he was sick?

MOTHER What?

MICK I dunno. I've been thinking about it for a while.

Beat.

MOTHER Well... Around Easter time is when he first realised something was wrong, which would have been what, a year and a half before he died? Because we were on holiday in Donegal, in Jackson's, you remember Jackson's hotel in

Ballybofey, we were there, and we were swimming in the pool. I mean I was, about seven...eight months pregnant at the time so I was just floating around in the pool, the big fat heap that I was. And he was in the pool and he couldn't lift his arm. Couldn't lift his arm to make a stroke. And I gave off stink to him. I says, "in the name of god Mickey when was the last time you were swimming? You're not fit, join the gym!" But he was obviously worried. He obviously knew the feeling he had in the arm, it wasn't right, you know.

MICK And that's when he started going to the doctors?

MOTHER Yes. Started going to the doctors and they kept doing all these tests for everything. Diabetes. Cancer. Whatever else. And they all kept coming back negative, which was great you know, but at the same time we were getting worried. Because the energy was draining from him and he was tired all the time, and no one seemed to know what was wrong. He was finally diagnosed the following February. Thursday 12th February. That was it, because then two days later was the 14th. Not a particularly joyful Valentine's Day, the Saturday. But they brought us in. Brought us both in. The doctor said they wanted to admit him, but only for more tests. And your dad just says to him, "Is it motor neurone disease?", cos I think he kinda knew and the doctor just said, "We need to do more tests". So Mickey plagued him. And plagued him. And plagued him. But the doctor wouldn't say. Even though it was pretty obvious because the junior doctor was sitting crying. Awk, she was only a young one, but she was, she was turned away and she was in tears. And your dad kept saying, "Is it motor neurone? Is it motor neurone?" He says, "We don't know we have to do more tests." Then eventually Micky turned around and says, "In your *opinion*, is it motor neurone disease?", and he says, "Yeah." *(beat)* I was just sitting there. Rubbing his back. I remember sitting there rubbing his back. Then he turns to me and he says, "Would you stop rubbing my back!" But I didn't know what else to do.

MICK I think I need to go to the doctor.

MOTHER What? What's wrong with you?

MICK I have a swelling on my testicle.

Beat.

MOTHER Right. We'll get that sorted.

Change.

DOCTOR Right, Michael. Thanks very much for coming in today. What we'll do is, if you want to go behind the screen there and get yourself sorted, I'll put some gloves on and see what I can feel. Don't be getting yourself worried. There's a lot of things it could be. So if you want to just nip behind the screen there and let me know when you're ready. Ok?

MICK Grand. *(mimes taking out massive ball)* Yep. That's me.

DOCTOR *(opens curtain with a look of shock)* Right. I see the swelling there. Obviously. Before I even touch it. Right. Do you mind if I? *(feels ball)* Gosh! Feel the weight of that. You've been carrying that around have you? Right. Phew! We really need to get you in for an ultrasound.

Change.

MICK *(to audience)* I hate hospitals. The beeps, the coughs, the shouts. The waiting. Mum gets a coffee in a small beige cup from the hospital vending machine. Smells like hot Weetabix. Was she annoyed at me for not telling her sooner? I wanted to tell to her. But the whole thing had become so tangled up with wanking that I felt like I couldn't. So we sit there in silence, surrounded by all these pregnant women, who are ushered one by one into the scanning rooms by a nurse who scuttles around like a flustered chicken.

NURSE That's it. Follow me now. It's just through here, just through here, just through there, just through there.

MICK Mum? How did Dad cope with it all? After he was diagnosed?

MOTHER Well… It was hard. I'm not going to lie to you, it was hard. He tried. He did try. He did everything he could. He fought. Went to all sorts of… Well quacks, really, who filled him full of God knows what, which wouldn't've been like Mickey. He was very much "Whatever the doctors say". But you get desperate… *(laughs)* and then the gym phoned me, remember I told him to go join a gym? Well they said to me, "You've not used the gym", and Mickey says to me that I might as well go. I says, "Mickey, I'm not leaving you." And he says, "No, you go." Cos, he'd been reading somewhere that if I physically worked my muscles, but mentally thought of his muscles, then that could help. So I was going to the gym like a mad thing…of course I get back home and he says, "It didn't work, you weren't going hard enough." *(laughs)* Ah no, he just…adjusted. Didn't drive, obviously. He had to sit at the front seat in Mass so he hadn't far to go for communion. He couldn't use his razor any more so I had to get him one of those electric ones.

MICK Yeah. I remember that.

MOTHER Do you?

NURSE Michael?

MICK *(to audience)* Chicken Little had finally reached my name on the clipboard.

NURSE That's it, just through here, just through here. So if you just want to take a wee seat there, I'll get you shaved.

MICK Shaved?

NURSE Yes. For the gel. You need to be shaved.

> **NURSE** *uses electric razor, it buzzes loudly.*

MICK *(to audience)* I look at my freshly shorn ball. It was hard to see through the wispy ginger fuzz before, but it's really big. It pulls the skin taut. Stretched out like a water balloon.

ULTRASOUND MAN It always looks bigger when it's shaved.

MICK *(startled)* What?

ULTRASOUND MAN How's it going, Michael? I'll be your technician today. Now, I'm not a doctor, so I'll not be giving a diagnosis. What I will do is perform the scan and then pass that information over to the doctor. That alright? Good. Now...let's have a look at what we can see.

"ALSO SPRACH ZARATHUSTRA" from 2001: A Space Odyssey *plays as* MICK *stares at the ultrasound.*

MICK *(to audience)* There it is. Proper ultrasound image. Like a baby. Except this baby has no limbs or face. It's just a big boiled egg. My left nut.

So what is it?

ULTRASOUND MAN Do you mean a boy or a girl?

MICK No! Like...what is it?

ULTRASOUND MAN Ah no, as I said, I can't say anything.

MICK But you must have seen hundreds of these. Please! What is it?

ULTRASOUND MAN I can't be saying.

MICK In your *opinion*, what is it?

Pause.

ULTRASOUND MAN In my *opinion*? Huh... *(beat)* In my *opinion*, you've to wait for the doctor!

MICK *(to audience)* And he leaves. I'm sitting there with a box of tissues to clean myself up. *(to testicle)* Why won't they tell me what you are? I waited for years before telling anyone about you. And now they won't tell me anything. When Dad felt sick, he went straight to the doctor and he

---

* A licence to produce MY LEFT NUT does not include a performance licence for "ALSO SPRACH ZARATHUSTRA". For further information, please see Music Use Note on page v.

still died. He wasn't sitting there with an obvious warning sign like you for years. I'm just a coward.

Text alert.

It's Tommy. *(reads)* "T-minus six hours till party time."

Change.

MICK *slowly takes of his tie and his school shirt and puts on a different shirt for the party. He styles his hair.*

(to audience) Really don't want to go tonight, but a free gaff is a free gaff... That was enough to get me onto the 8A bus, and get off in...

Change.

BUS DRIVER Erinvale! Last stop!

MICK   *(to audience)* The edge of a Loyalist Estate. I keep my head down and walk on. Passing through Finaghy Cross roads. Entering into West Belfast. I walk the final mile to Tommy's house on Blacks Road. I round the corner of his cul-de-sac and see the light streaming from every window of the semi-detached, spilling out onto the well-kept garden out front. I see the outlines of people inside; drinking, dancing, having fun. I shouldn't've come. I'll just go in. I'll not drink. I'll show my face for five minutes and then head on. I'll not go mental or anything.

Change.

TOMMY Yeeeeooooo what's happenin', Mick?! Welcome to Chez Tommy! One bottle of Frosty Jack's for you. Down it! Down it! Down it!

TOMMY *hands* MICK *a bottle.* MICK *takes it, shrugs, and downs it.*

MICK ARRGHERGUHUGHTGHEHGHGFHD!!!!!!

Change.

MICK *dances in montage to suitable 2000s party music.*

Change.

(to audience) Need a breather. Move into the kitchen, and there's Conor, putting the world to rights.

CONOR Look, it's not a question of Ireland being united or not. The fact is, in ten years, Ireland and the UK will be so integrated into the European Union, that the Irish border question will be made irrelevant...

NIALL THE NUTTER FUCK OFF!

CONOR Don't come crying to me when we're all speaking Esperanto! Saluton, Mick! Want some vodko?

MICK *(to audience)* And Conor's culchie cousin danders over. Checkered shirt tucked into high-waisted jeans. And enough Brylcreem to style an army.

CAHIL Ah well, Cyonor! This is some gathering hai! Vodkie?! Don't mind if I do! Fill her up there. Now we're sucking diesel! *(to the side)* Girls! Would yis join me for a dance?!

MICK *(to audience)* And he walks off with a girl on each arm! While me and Conor look on, dumbfounded. Until...

TOMMY *(shouts)* Conor, your cousins a disgrace! He's only gone and changed the music! It took me two weeks to download all them songs off LimeWire: 8 o'clock to 9.30, crowd-pleasers. 9.30 to 10.45, South American hip-hop. 10.45 to late – Soviet Dance anthems. And for those still standing at the end, a special treat. Nothing but Pure. French. Cabaret.

CONOR You have an eclectic taste in music, Tommy.

TOMMY Conor, we're not even half-way through South American hip-hop and he's in there line-dancing to Cotton Eye Fuckin-Joe!

Change.

CAHIL *dances to Rednex, "**COTTON EYE JOE**".**

***Change**.*

How are we supposed to work our "group dynamics" when culchie boy's stealing all the women? Even the Stallion can't compete with that!

CONOR Yeoooo! Big Dick Mick! Big Dick Mick!

MICK Shut up, lads! Would you stop it with that stallion crap! Give me that vodka! *(swig)*

TOMMY Woah, Mick. I think maybe you should take it easy.

MICK Well do you wanna know what I think? *(He swigs.)* I think... *(He swigs.)* I think... I think... I think... *(He swigs.)* I think I'm gonna boke.

TOMMY Ah right right! Ehhhh! The downstairs bog, Mick. The downstairs bog!

MICK *stumbles to the downstairs bog. He reaches a door and, relieved, turns the handle.*

NIALL THE NUTTER FUCK OFF! I'M DOING A POO!

Panic.

TOMMY The front door! The front door!

MICK *stumbles towards the front door.*

***Change**.*

MICK *enters slow motion as he reaches towards the door with Edith Piaf's **"NON, JE NE REGRETTE RIEN"**** playing. He reaches for the door handle, happy and triumphant. At the last minute his stomach wretches and he vomits everywhere in slow motion as the song climaxes.*

---

*/** A licence to produce MY LEFT NUT does not include a performance licence for "COTTON EYE JOY" or "NON, JE NE REGRETTE RIEN". For further information, please see Music Use Note on page v.

Change.

MICK Lying in a puddle of vomit. In Tommy's Da's front garden. I feel like a piece of shit.

TOMMY Jesus, Mick! You could boke for Ireland. Come on! Up you get, up you get. *(goes to pick up* MICK*)* Woooow! Down you go, down you go. Here, wait till you see this. *(*TOMMY *takes a cigar from his pocket.)*

MICK Where'd you get a cigar?

TOMMY Nicked it from my da. *(lights and takes drag)* You gotta have a cigar at a house party, Mick. It's classy. *(coughs)* Here, what was all that about inside? Seriously, Mick. It's not like you to be getting on like that. What's wrong?

MICK What's wrong?

TOMMY What's wrong?

MICK What's wrong?

TOMMY What's wrong?!

MICK What's wrong?!

TOMMY Aye, what's wrong?!!

MICK What's wrong?! I'VE GOT BALL CANCER!

Pause.

TOMMY Shit. You gonna die?

MICK Dunno.

TOMMY Fuck. You want a beer?

MICK Aye.

TOMMY Right.

Change.

SIOBHAN Tommy! Are you outside with Mick? I'm gonna smack that wee dick! He gat vomit all over my bag!

TOMMY Ummm...no, you can't do that.

SIOBHAN Why nat?!

TOMMY Shhhh! Cos...cos...cos he's got cancer.

SIOBHAN He's got wha? OH MUMMY!

MICK And the news spreads through the party like wildfire!

SIOBHAN Mick's got cancer!

NIAL THE NUTTER Mick's getting his balls chopped off!

MARY Mick has a week to live!

CAHIL Mick's dead!

MARY No no, Mick's not dead!

CAHIL Mick's got cancer!

> *Change.*

CONOR Have you got cancer?

MICK Alright, Conor. Umm maybe.

CONOR Maybe? Mick, everyone's going mental in there. The party's a complete shit-show. Have you got cancer?

MICK Ach, Conor. I'm not a stallion, Ok? I've got a swelling on my testicle...but they won't tell me what it is.

CONOR So... *(beat)* you don't have a big dick?

MICK Well it's not tiny or anything.

CONOR Thank fuck! Do you have any idea how pathetic me and Tommy felt next to you and your massive schlong. That's the best news I've heard all week. (**CONOR** *looks at the ball.*) So that's like a swelling? Jesus. Why didn't you tell us?

MICK I dunno.

> *A car's headlights sweep across the stage with screeching brakes sound effects.*

(to audience) And we're blinded by headlights of a silver Vauxhall, pulling up into the driveway. Tommy's parents step out with a look of horror.

TOMMY'S DA What's this?! Some wee fecker has thrown up all over my petunias! TOMMMYYY! YOU WEE BASTARD!

CONOR Come on Mick. We gotta get out here! Tommy's Da's in the 'RA!!!

MICK *(to audience)* We hoof it up the street, sprint through Ladybrook, 'round to the Andytown Road and flag down a black taxi. I feel so much better about everything. I mean... I ruined Tommy's party. I told everyone I have cancer. But the lads know about the ball. Back into the house.

Change.

(to audience) Someone's up. And I'm still kinda drunk. And covered in vomit. I look in. And there's Mum. Asleep on the couch. Ironing board still up in front of the flickering TV. I turn it off at the wall and pick up her book, which had fallen on the floor: "Raising Boys by Steve Biddulph: Why Boys Are Different – and How to Help Them Become Happy and Well-Balanced Men". I place it carefully on the sofa and sneak up to bed.

Change.

MAURICE Mick?

MICK Yeah, Maurice.

MAURICE Do you smell vomit?

Change.

MICK *(to audience)* Back in the hospital with Mum. Finally going to find out what's wrong.

Mum? What was it like when Dad actually died?

MOTHER Ah now, Michael. Don't be thinking about that now!

MICK No. I want to know.

MOTHER Well. He died on a Thursday. It must have been the weekend before, everyone had been in to see him, you know friends and family and all that, and he says to me, "Pauline, it's not looking good, they're all coming to see me." *(laughs)* So then I got the doctor out. The consultant, because the GP hadn't a clue. And your man was very good, actually he came out to the house after, you know, he was finished in hospital and he checked him out and all and stuff. And he gave him a drip, you know, just for fluids and all. But he didn't have a stand for it, so he hung it on a picture hook on the wall. He was just that sort of being, you know. And then when he was leaving I said to him, "Well you know, how long do you think" and he says, "Days." So I phoned Mummy. I phoned your granny and told her what the doctor said and she said, "Pauline, it's time to let him go." But I wasn't ready. So I lay just in bed with him. And I was there. I had my arms around him and it was the doctor then that said, "He's gone." And I'm there like, "How do you know? How do you know?" He says, "No Pauline. He is." He just. He just slipped away. I mean...in terms of suffering and all that, yes, he did suffer, but only because he knew he was leaving us. But. It could have been a lot worse. It could have been a lot worse. It was just a lovely way that he just...he just...lay. I mean I was in bed with him. Holding him when he died. He was in his own bed and everybody 'round him. He's up there. He's up there. We're not with him. But he's up there.

NURSE Michael? The doctor is ready for you now.

MOTHER On you go, Michael, I'll be here.

DOCTOR Well, Michael. Thanks for coming in. So. I've had a look at your scans and I can tell you what's wrong. *(beat)* It's fluid.

MICK Fluid?

DOCTOR Fluid.

MICK *(to audience)* Fluid! It's just fluid! It is just a big water balloon after all! I'm not going to die! Because I don't have cancer. I've got...what have I got?

DOCTOR It's called a hydrocele. Simply a build-up of fluid caused by a defective absorbing membrane. It's very common... Admittedly, I've never seen one this size before. But all perfectly harmless. We have two options. We can insert a needle and let it drain out. The only problem there is that it might come back, in which case, we'd have to keep needling it every year or so. Or we can go in surgically, and sort it out for good.

MICK *(to audience)* The image flashes through my brain of a giant needle piercing my balls every year for the rest of my life.

Surgery! Surgery's good.

DOCTOR Lovely. Count backwards from ten...

Change.

MICK Nine...eight...seven...

The opening music to the Sega Mega Drive/Genesis game Streets of Rage* plays.

(to audience) I float away as my consciousness is stolen by the anaesthetic gas... This body was once a happy peaceful place...until one day. A powerful secret swelling took over. The body has become a centre of illness and malady where no one is safe. Amid this turmoil, a group of determined young doctors has sworn to take out the ball. They are willing to risk anything, even their lives...on the...NUTS OF RAGE.

(to audience) I see myself as a pixelated doctor. Armed with scalpel and knife, I take on the demonic testicle in front of me. Just as I'm about to hit it, one final blow, the pixelated world explodes in a Technicolor burst of neon blocks. And

---

* A licence to produce MY LEFT NUT does not include a performance licence for "STREETS OF RAGE". For further information, please see Music Use Note on page v.

I find myself back in my living room. Watching eight-year-old me playing Streets of Rage in front of the TV. I look at him. He's fully absorbed in the screen. Shutting himself off to everything going on around him. Lost. I think back to my father's funeral.

YOUNG MICK "It's not my dad anyway. It's just a body. Dad's away on."

MICK *(to audience)* My father. Michael Damien Thaddeus Campbell. Is dead. He's not coming back. He's never going to talk to me about politics or catch me having a house party. But that's grand. My mum can do that. And she can tell me stories about him and I'll share those stories with people and he'll live there. And that's not as good as him living here. Today. With me now. But it's a damn sight better than a kick in the balls. And I watch my father's coffin being lowered into the ground. And I don't feel happy. But I don't feel sad. I just feel.

Change.

(to audience) And I awake. With...two tiny testicles! I have to stop...you know... *(makes masturbating motion)* for a while. But that's out of physical pain rather than existential dread. I had to re-seed Tommy's da's front garden. Went and bought grass seed and everything. Funnily enough, he already had loads of nitrate fertiliser. I come home from Tommy's. Dump the grass seed in the garage and nip in the back door. And there's Mum. White as a sheet.

MOTHER Was that you that just came round the back there?

MICK Aye. Who else would it be?

MOTHER Oh my God. I near had the fright of my life. I could have sworn you were Mickey. I thought it was your father. I thought he'd come home. I don't know what it was about you, but you were just the double of him. The absolute spit of him.

MICK How did *you* do it, Mum? How did you cope when Dad died, with all of us?

MOTHER How did I cope? Well... I just coped. Actually, I did have a feeling. I thought I'd not be able to cope. "I'll not be able to cope." ...You know, he was so into all four of you. Everyone kept saying, "You're so lucky to have them. You're so lucky to have the kids, Pauline. You're so lucky to have them", and I kept thinking, "I wish I had none of yous." It was the burden. The responsibility. It wasn't just raising you. It was raising you for him. That was all he wanted at the end. "Make sure you're there for them Pauline. Make sure you're there for them." And I tried. Lord knows I tried. I could never bring him back for you, but I could do everything else. I suppose I coped all right in the end.

MICK You coped brilliantly, Mum. Thanks. For everything.

MOTHER He was a great man. I must say.

MICK I know.

MOTHER Right. Go shower, would you? You're stinking of fertiliser! I had the immersion on for you coming home, so there should be plenty of hot water.

MICK Thanks, Mum. You're too good.

MICK *produces an electric razor and turns it on. It buzzes loudly.*

MICK *shaves with a smile on his face, as AC/DC* **"BIG BALLS"*** *plays.*

Blackout.

---

* A licence to produce MY LEFT NUT does not include a performance licence for "BIG BALLS". For further information, please see Music Use Note on page v.

PROPS/LIGHTNING/SOUND EFFECTS

Set: A modified black Ikea Stefan chair

Props: None

Costume: White shirt, black trousers, old trainers, school tie, blue shirt, pale T-shirt

Lighting: Cold wash / Warm wash / Spotlight special / coloured LEDs for full stage wash (if not using LEDs – green, magenta, blue, red)

VISIT THE SAMUEL FRENCH BOOKSHOP AT THE ROYAL COURT THEATRE

Browse plays and theatre books, get expert advice and enjoy a coffee

Samuel French Bookshop
Royal Court Theatre
Sloane Square
London
SW1W 8AS
020 7565 5024

Shop from thousands of titles on our website

 samuelfrench.co.uk

 samuelfrenchltd

 samuel french uk

.

Lightning Source UK Ltd.
Milton Keynes UK
UKHW021821090819
347719UK00006B/196/P

9 780573 116414